T0195597

MATH
EXTENSION UNITS

Written by Judy Leimbach and Kathy Leimbach
Illustrated by Mary Lou Johnson

Place Value • Time and Measurement • Problem Solving • Money

First published in 2005 by Prufrock Press Inc.

Published in 2021 by Routledge
605 Third Avenue, New York, NY 10017
2 Park Square, Milton Park, Abingdon, Oxon OX14 4RN

Routledge is an imprint of the Taylor & Francis Group, an informa business

ISBN: 9781593630997 (pbk)

DOI: 10.4324/9781003236474

Contents

Math Extension Units
(Book 1, Grades 2-3)

Unit	Common Core State Standards in Math
Place Value	2.NBT.A Understand place value. 2.NBT.B Use place value understanding and properties of operations to add and subtract. 4.NBT.A Generalize place value understanding for multi-digit whole numbers.
Problem Solving and Computational Application	2.OA.A Represent and solve problems involving addition and subtraction. 2.OA.B Add and subtract within 20. 2.OA.C Work with equal groups of objects to gain foundations for multiplication. 2.NBT.B Use place value understanding and properties of operations to add and subtract. 2.MD.C Work with time and money. 3.OA.A Represent and solve problems involving multiplication and division. 3.OA.B Understand properties of multiplication and the relationship between multiplication and division. 3.OA.D Solve problems involving the four operations, and identify and explain patterns in arithmetic. 3.MD.A Solve problems involving measurement and estimation. 4.MD.A Solve problems involving measurement and conversion of measurements.
Money	2.OA.A Represent and solve problems involving addition and subtraction. 2.OA.B Add and subtract within 20. 2.MD.C Work with time and money. 3.MD.A Solve problems involving measurement and estimation. 4.MD.A Solve problems involving measurement and conversion of measurements.
Time and Measurement	2.OA.A Represent and solve problems involving addition and subtraction. 2.OA.B Add and subtract within 20. 2.MD.C Work with time and money. 3.NF.A Develop understanding of fractions as numbers. 3.MD.A Solve problems involving measurement and estimation. 4.MD.A Solve problems involving measurement and conversion of measurements. 6.NS.C Apply and extend previous understandings of numbers to the system of rational numbers.

Key:

OA = Operations & Algebraic Thinking; NBT = Number & Operations in Base Ten; NF = Number & Operations–Fractions; MD =

Information for the Instructor

The purpose of this book is to help busy classroom teachers provide for those students who quickly grasp the mathematical concepts being taught and are ready to move on to more challenging material. The extension activities provided in the four units of this book will help students expand their knowledge in each area and give them opportunities to apply their skills in a variety of different ways. The units include challenging activities that will require higher-level thinking and will broaden students' problem solving skills.

Our most able students should be encouraged to stretch their thinking, to expand their learning, and to develop perseverance. It is the teacher's responsibility to provide them with opportunities to do so and to encourage them in their efforts. These units provide a way for teachers to easily offer these kinds of educational experiences for their able math students.

How to Use the Units

The materials in this book may be used for the whole class or as extension units for individuals or small groups. The units were designed primarily to meet the needs of students who learn quickly, work at a fast pace, and are capable of going beyond the regular mathematics curriculum at their grade level.

The units in this book correspond to topics usually included in the primary grade mathematics curriculum. Each unit provides meaningful extension activities that advanced math students could work on while their classmates are mastering the more basic concepts. The pages in each section can be compiled into a packet with the Assignment Sheet as the cover page and given to each student to work on independently. The units can also be arranged in a math center with each student having an individual folder, using the Assignment Sheet to record progress.

Extension Units

Place Value

Students should have a basic understanding of our number system before they begin this unit. The activities in this unit include:
- recognizing the value of each digit in a number
- translating from verbal to numerical representations
- using logic and a knowledge of place value to find a mystery number
- writing numbers greater than one thousand
- adding numbers greater than one thousand

- ordering large numbers.

Problem Solving and Computational Application

Before beginning this unit, students should have good basic computational skills (addition and subtraction), as they will be asked to use these skills in different problem solving situations. Each lesson presents a scenario and four or five problems related to this scenario. Most of the problems require students to do more than simple calculations. They usually will need to choose a strategy for solving the problem and use more than one set of computations to arrive at each answer.

Money

Before beginning this unit, students should know the value of the different coins and a dollar. Besides writing and counting money, they will be asked to:
- supply different combinations of coins to equal given amounts of money
- use logic to determine the number of each coin needed to satisfy the conditions given (number of coins and amount)
- solve problems involving money.

Time and Measurement

This unit includes three different concepts; time, temperature, and liquid measurement. The lessons on time deal with:
- reading both analog and digital clocks
- solving problems involving time
- reading a monthly calendar
- reading a yearly calendar.

The lessons on measurement include both lessons on temperature and lessons on liquid measurement. Students will be asked to:
- add and subtract temperatures above and below zero
- figure equivalent measurements of gallons, quarts, pints and cups
- solve problems using units of liquid measurement.

Certificate of Achievement

This is to certify that _____

has exercised great skill and diligence and has

successfully completed the math unit on

_____

The unit was completed and checked on _____

Congratulations on a job well done!

Comments

_____

_____

_____

_____

_____
Teacher's signature

Assignment Sheet

Name _____

I began this unit on place value on _____ (date)

Mark off each activity after you have completed it and after it has been checked. Hand in all pages when you finish the unit.

Lesson	Completed	Checked
1. Importance of Place	_____	_____
2. Understanding Place Value	_____	_____
3. Different Ways	_____	_____
4. Number Pyramid	_____	_____
5. Place Value Scramble	_____	_____
6. Finding Mystery Numbers	_____	_____
7. What's My Mystery Number? (1-20)	_____	_____
8. What's My Mystery Number? (20-99)	_____	_____
9. What's My Mystery Number? (100-999)	_____	_____
10. Really Big Numbers	_____	_____
11. More or Less	_____	_____
12. Largest to Smallest	_____	_____

I completed this unit on _____ (date).

Importance of Place

Name _____

1. In our decimal number system
   it is very important where each
   numeral is placed. Look at
   where the numeral 5 is placed
   in each of the examples below.

    a. 3,21**5**   b. 7,**5**46   c. 8,3**5**0   d. **5**,927

In which number does the 5 equal 500? _____

In which number does the 5 equal 5,000? _____

In which number does the 5 equal 50? _____

2. For each number on the left, write what each digit stands for.

    a. **4,815**   The 4 equals ___4,000___ The 8 equals_____

                  The 1 equals ___10___ The 5 equals_____

    b. **7,392**   The 9 equals_____ The 7 equals_____

                  The 2 equals_____ The 3 equals_____

    c. **2,643**   The 3 equals_____ The 4 equals_____

                  The 6 equals_____ The 2 equals_____

    d. **8,270**   The 2 equals_____ The 0 equals_____

                  The 8 equals_____ The 7 equals_____

    e. **4,509**   The 4 equals_____ The 5 equals_____

                  The 0 equals_____ The 9 equals_____

Understanding Place Value

Name _____

5,264	3,782	2,351
1,900	4,625	6,043
8,136	2,907	5,624
1,879	7,418	9,590

Use the numbers in the box above to answer these questions.

1. Which number has a 4 in the tens place? _____

2. Which number has 0 hundreds? _____

3. Which number has 8 thousands? _____

4. Which number has 8 hundreds? _____

5. Which of the numbers with 2 in the thousands place is larger? _____

6. Which numbers have 5 thousands and 4 ones? _____

7. Which number has 4 thousands? _____

8. Which number has 4 hundreds? _____

9. Which numbers have 9 hundreds and 0 tens? _____

10. Which number equals 3,000 + 700 + 80 + 2? _____

11. Which is the smallest number? _____

12. Which is the largest number? _____

13. Which numbers have an even number in the thousands place? _____

_____

Different Ways

Name _____

You can use the four numerals 2, 7, 5, and 9 to write several different numbers. Some of the numbers you can write are 5,793, 2,953, 9,375 and 7,952. There are many other numbers you could write using these same four digits.

1. Write the smallest number you can using 5, 7, 2, and 9. _____

   Write the largest number. _____

2. Write the largest number you can using 3, 1, 7, and 5. _____

   Write the smallest number. _____

3. Write six different numbers using 6, 3, and 5. _____

   _____

4. Write four numbers with odd numerals in the hundreds and ones places using 4, 3, 7, and 6.

   _____

5. Write six numbers that are larger than 5,000 using 3, 0, 5, and 2.

   _____   _____   _____

   _____   _____   _____

Number Pyramid

Name _____

Write each number in the correct block on the pyramid.

1. 4 hundreds, 1 ten, 3 ones
2. 4 hundreds, 3 tens, 2 ones
3. 4 thousands, 8 hundreds, 6 tens, 7 ones
4. 1 thousand, 9 hundreds, 3 tens, 7 ones
5. 3 hundreds, 4 tens, 7 ones
6. 2 tens, 8 ones
7. 1 thousand, 8 hundreds, 6 tens, 0 ones
8. 4 hundreds, 9 tens, 5 ones
9. 6 thousands, 3 hundreds, 3 tens, 6 ones
10. 7 hundreds, 9 tens, 7 ones
11. 8 tens, 3 ones
12. 3 hundreds, 0 tens, 2 ones
13. 3 thousands, 9 hundreds, 6 tens, 5 ones
14. 9 hundreds, 0 tens, 2 ones
15. 1 thousands, 5 hundred, 1 tens, 3 ones

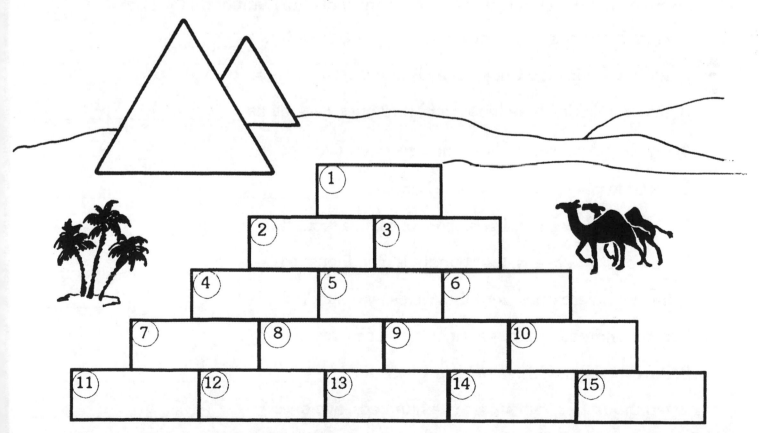

PLACE VALUE SCRAMBLE

Name _____

The number 4,286 would usually be written out as
four thousands, two hundreds, eight tens and **six ones**

But it could be scrambled and written out as
eight tens, four thousands, six ones and *two hundreds*

Both equal **4,286.**

Unscramble the numbers written below and write the number on the line.

1. eight hundreds, nine ones, one thousand, three tens = _____

2. six tens, four thousands, seven hundreds, two ones = _____

3. five hundreds, three thousands, zero ones, seven tens = _____

4. one hundred, seven thousands, six ones, two tens = _____

5. six thousands, five ones, nine hundreds = _____

6. four tens, three hundreds, eight ones, five thousands = _____

7. one one, three tens, four hundreds, two thousands = _____

8. five tens, zero ones, zero thousands, two hundreds = _____

9. two hundreds, five ones, eight thousands, one ten = _____

10. nine thousands, three ones, two tens = _____

11. ten thousands, two tens, three hundreds, five ones = _____

Finding Mystery Numbers

Name _____

Robbie is thinking of an odd number between 5 and 15.
Write all the possible answers.

5 _____ _____ _____ _____ 15

Clues

His number has 2 digits. Cross out the numbers that do not have 2 digits.
The two digits are the same. Circle the number Robbie is thinking of.

Find the mystery numbers below. Write all the possible answers. As you read the clues, cross out the wrong answers and circle the right ones.

1. Ramon is thinking of an even number that is more than 20 and less than 40.
   Clues
   • *The digit in tens place is an odd number.*
   • *The sum of the digits is 7.*
   What is his number? _____

2. Tonja is thinking of a 2-digit number with a 0 in the ones place.
   Clues
   • *The digit in tens place is an even number.*
   • *It is the largest number that fits the clues.*
   What is her number? _____

3. Matthew is thinking of a 3 digit number less than 111.
   Clues
   • *Two of the digits are the same.*
   • *There is a one in the tens place.*
   What is his number? _____

What's My Mystery Number?
Numbers 1 - 20

Name _____

All of the mystery numbers below are between 1 and 20. Use the clues to find each mystery number.

1. The mystery number is an even number.
   - It has only one digit.
   - It can be divided into groups of 3.
   The mystery number is _____

2. The mystery number is an odd number.
   - It has two digits.
   - The digits are the same.
   The mystery number is _____

3. The mystery number is an even number.
   - It has two digits.
   - The digit in tens place is 5 less than the digit in ones place.
   The mystery number is _____

4. The mystery number is an odd number.
   - It has a 3 in the ones place.
   - It is less than 12.
   The mystery number is _____

5. The mystery number is an even number.
   - It has two digits.
   - The digit in ones place is 3 more than digit in tens place.
   The mystery number is _____

6. The mystery number is an even number.
   - It has two digits.
   - The digit in ones place is 7 more than the digit in tens place.
   The mystery number is _____

What's My Mystery Number?
Numbers 20 - 99

Name _____

All of the mystery numbers below are between 20 and 99.
Use the clues to find each mystery number.

1. The mystery number is an even number.
   • The digit in tens place is half the digit in ones place.
   • The sum of the digits is 12.
   The mystery number is _____

2. The mystery number is an odd number.
   • The digit in tens place equals the digit in ones place.
   • The sum of the digits is more than 10 and less than 15.
   The mystery number is _____

3. The mystery number is an even number less than 50.
   • The digit in tens place is odd.
   • The sum of the digits is 9.
   • The digit in tens place is half the digit in the ones place.
   The mystery number is _____

4. The mystery number is an even number.
   • Half of the digit in tens place is 3.
   • The sum of the digits is 10.
   The mystery number is _____

5. The mystery number is an even number.
   • The digit in tens place is 3 more than the digit in ones place.
   • The sum of the digits is less than 5.
   The mystery number is _____

6. Both digits in the mystery number are odd numbers.
   • The digit in tens place is 4 more than the digit in ones place.
   • It is the largest number that fits the clues.
   The mystery number is _____

What's My Mystery Number?
Numbers 100 - 999

Name _____

All of the mystery numbers below are between 100 and 999. Use the clues to find each mystery number.

1. The mystery number is an odd number.
   - The digit in tens place equals the digit in ones place.
   - The sum of the digits is 11.
   - The number is less than 500.
   The mystery number is _____

2. The mystery number has three even digits.
   - The digit in the tens place is 2 less than the digit in hundreds place and 2 more than the digit in ones place.
   - The sum of the digits is 12.
   The mystery number is _____

3. The mystery number is an odd number.
   - The sum of the digits is 18.
   - One of the digits is zero.
   The mystery number is _____

4. The mystery number is an even number.
   - The digit in ones place is 1 more than the digit in tens place.
   - The digit in tens place is 1 more than the digit in hundreds place.
   - The sum of the digits is less than 15.
   The mystery number is _____

16

Really Big Numbers

Name _____

For numbers over 1,000 a comma separates the thousands from the rest of the number (the hundreds, tens, and ones).

The first number to the left of the comma tells us how many **thousands**. The next number to the left tells us how many **ten thousands**. The next number to the left tells us how many **hundred thousands**.

hundred thousands	ten thousands	thousands	,	hundreds	tens	ones

When we read really big numbers, the comma tells us to say "thousand." So we read **250,162** as *two hundred fifty* **thousand**, *one hundred sixty-two*.

195,267	210,175	304,690	562,068

Use the numbers in the box above to answer these questions.

1. Which number has nine ten thousands?_____

2. Which number has no ten thousands?_____

3. Which number has no thousands?_____

4. Which number has five hundred thousands? _____

Write the following numbers.

5. two hundred thirty-one thousand, two hundred fifty _____

6. twenty-nine thousand, five hundred forty-two _____

7. seven hundred and five thousand, one hundred_____

8. eight thousand, seventy-five _____

More or Less

Name _____

1. Use 4, 1, 3, 0, 2, and 5 to write four numbers greater than 500,000.

_____   _____   _____   _____

Circle the number that is the largest.

2. Use 5, 7, 3, 6, 0, and 9 to write four numbers less than 500,000.

_____   _____   _____   _____

Circle the number that is less than the other three.

3. Write the number that is

a. 1,000 more than 5,280 _____

b. 200 less than 1,962 _____

c. 2,000 more than 13,600 _____

d. 10,000 less than 85,450 _____

e. 30,000 more than 125,680 _____

f. 100,000 less than 585,000 _____

g. 500,000 more than 290,595 _____

h. 110 less than 750,860 _____

i. 110,000 more than 345,675 _____

j. 100,100 more than 492,400 _____

k. 111,111 less than 895,764 _____

l. 222,222 more than 341,526 _____

Bonus What is 100,000 more than 900,000? _____

Largest to Smallest

Name _____

Ski down the slope by putting the largest number from the box at the top of the hill. Then write the next largest number in the next box down the ski slope. Finish with the smallest number at the bottom of the slope.

| 437,289 | 257,145 | 23,794 | 14,294 |
| 310,712 | 311,712 | 527,289 | 14,393 |

Assignment Sheet

Name _____

I began this unit on problem solving on _____ (date).

Mark off each activity after you have completed it and after it has been checked. Hand in all pages when you finish the unit.

Lesson	Completed	Checked
1. Jessie's Valentine Party	_____	_____
2. The Amusement Park	_____	_____
3. Trip to the Farm	_____	_____
4. A Day at the Beach	_____	_____
5. George's Birthday Party	_____	_____
6. Playing Darts	_____	_____
7. Reading Club	_____	_____
8. Book Store Sale	_____	_____
9. Collection Fair	_____	_____
10. Fast Food	_____	_____
11. School Store	_____	_____
12. Speedy Delivery	_____	_____
13. Field Day	_____	_____

I completed the unit on _____ (date).

Jessie's Valentine Party

Name _____

Jessie invited 6 girls and 7 boys to her valentine party. They played games at the party, exchanged valentines, and had cake and ice cream. Everyone had fun.

1. Jessie's invitations came 6 in a package. How may packages of invitations did she need to buy?

   _____ packages

2. Each child at the party (including Jessie) got a party favor. The party favors came in packages of 8. She bought 2 packages. How many favors were left over?

   _____ favors

3. Four (4) of the children ate 2 scoops of ice cream with their cake. All of the others ate 1 scoop. How many scoops of ice cream were eaten?

   _____ scoops

4. The children at the party divided into two teams to play a ring toss game. Which team won and by how many points?

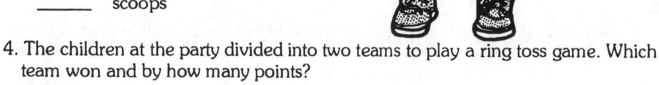

Team 1		Team 2	
Sally	10 points	Erin	10 points
Ben	15 points	Marty	15 points
Yuki	10 points	Charles	20 points
Brett	20 points	Laura	10 points
Scotty	10 points	Mike	15 points
Jolene	10 points	Sarah	20 points
Jessie	15 points	Tony	10 points

Team _____ won by _____ points

THE AMUSEMENT PARK

Name _____

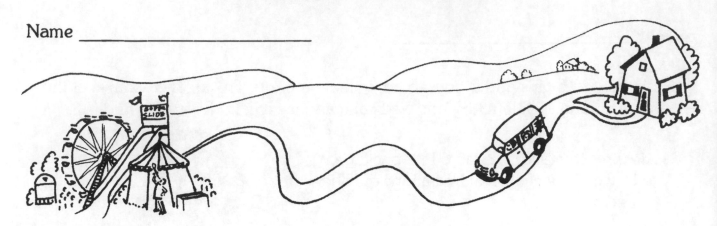

One day during their vacation, Kyle and Megan's mother and father took them to an amusement park. They went on rides, played some games, ate snacks, and saw a show. They had a great day!

1. The amusement park was 40 miles from their home. The drive took them 1 hour each way. They left home at 1:00 p.m. and got home at 9:00 p.m. How many hours did they spend at the park?

    _____ hours

2. The tickets for the amusement park cost $10 for adults and $7 for children. How much did it cost their family to get in the park?

    $_____

3. Kyle and Megan went on 6 rides together. Kyle went on 4 other rides with his dad and 2 with his mother. Megan went on 3 other rides with her dad and 4 with her mother. How many more rides did Megan go on than Kyle?

    _____ rides

4. Each of the children bought snacks to eat. This is what they cost.

Kyle's Snacks		Megan's Snacks	
Hamburger	$2.50	Hot Dog	$1.50
Fries	$1.00	Chips	.50
Soda	$1.00	Soda	$1.00
Popcorn	$1.00	Ice Cream	$1.00

Kyle spent how much more on snacks than Megan spent? $_____

Trip to the Farm

Name _____

In October the 13 boys and 11 girls in Mrs. Hastings' second grade class visited a farm. They did many fun things at the farm and had a wonderful day.

1. Each student picked an apple to eat from the basket. If there were 34 apples in the basket, how many were left after the students took their apples?

   _____apples

2. Next they fed the baby animals. There were 2 goats, 1 pony, 4 chickens, 1 duck, 2 geese, and 2 llamas. The farmer gave them 1/2 cup of food for each animal. How many cups of food did the farmer give the children?

   _____ cups

3. When they went on a hay ride there were 12 bales of hay on the wagon. If Mrs. Hastings, her class, and 5 parents sat on the bales of hay with 3 people sitting on each bale, how many other people could ride with them?

   _____ people

4. In the pumpkin field each child was allowed to pick 1 pumpkin. They weighed their pumpkins. The boys' pumpkins weighed 42 pounds altogether. The girls' pumpkins weighed 33 pounds. When Mrs. Hastings added her pumpkin, the total weight of their pumpkins was 85 pounds. How many pounds did Mrs. Hastings' pumpkin weigh?

   _____ pounds

A Day at the Beach

Name _____

Christina, Anna, Ali and their parents, Mr. and Mrs. Romano, spent the day at the beach.

1. Mr. and Mrs. Romano together found 14 shells. Ali found 6. Christina found 16 and Anna found 4. How many more will they need to find to have 50 shells altogether?

   _____ shells

2. Mr. Romano worked on his sand castle for 12 minutes, rested 5 minutes, then worked 4 more minutes. Mrs. Romano worked on her sand castle for 8 minutes, rested 3 minutes, then worked 12 minutes more. Who took the longest time to complete a sand castle and how many minutes longer?

   _____ took _____ minutes longer

3. Christina and Anna made a sand castle and decorated the four castle walls with shells. Christina put 5 shells on each wall. Anna put 8 shells on each wall. How many more shells did Anna use than Christina?

   _____ shells

4. Mrs. Romano packed a picnic lunch for the beach. She packed enough sandwiches so Mr. and Mrs. Romano would each have 11/2 sandwiches, Ali would have 1 sandwich, and the other two girls would each have 1/2 of a sandwich. How many slices of bread did she use to make the sandwiches?

   _____ slices

George's Birthday Party

Name _____

Marga and Gabriel were excited about their older brother George's sixteenth birthday. They helped their mother get ready for the party.

1. Marga was decorating the cake. She had 5 blue, 3 white, and 4 yellow candle holders. How many more holders would she need for the 16 candles?

_____ candle holders

2. George invited 5 of his friends to the party. His mother, Marga and Gabriel would be there also. If each person used 2 birthday napkins, how many napkins would be left from the 2 packages of 10 that his mother bought?

_____ napkins

3. George's party started at 5:00 p.m. They had to leave for the bowling alley at 6:15 p.m. If it took them 30 minutes to eat pizza, how much time was left to play video games and open presents before they left?

_____ minutes

4. George and his friends each had a large drink at the bowling alley. Large drinks cost $1.00 each. Marga and Gabriel each had a small drink that cost $.75 each. How much change did his mother get from $8.00?

$_____

PLAYING DARTS

Name _____

Tonya and Kevin played a game of darts. They each threw four darts in each round. They played three rounds. The charts below show where their darts landed in each round. Figure out each person's score and who won the game.

Black
Green
Blue
Yellow
Red
25
15
10
5
0

Tonya	Red	Yellow	Blue	Green	Black
Round 1	0	1	1	1	1
Round 2	1	0	2	1	0
Round 3	0	2	0	1	1

Tonya's score: rounds 1_____ 2_____ 3_____ Total_____

Kevin	Red	Yellow	Blue	Green	Black
Round 1	0	2	1	1	0
Round 2	0	1	0	2	1
Round 3	1	1	0	0	2

Kevin's score: rounds 1_____ 2_____ 3_____Total_____

The winner was _____

Bonus Problem

On the back make a chart to show all the possible ways you could score 50 points throwing four darts.

Reading Club

Name _____

The Pulaski School second graders formed a reading club. At the end of the month the students totaled the number of books they each read that month. Each child received a certificate and a special treat.

1. Valerie read 15 books in September, 25 books in October, and 12 books in November. How many more books will she have to read to read her goal of 72 books?

   _____ books

2. Todd's mother sent juice boxes for the March Reading Club's meeting. There were six juice boxes in each package. How many packages of juice did Todd's mom need for the 14 boys and 14 girls in the class?

   _____ packages   How many juice boxes were left? _____ boxes

3. Bill read 8 books in February and 15 books in March. In April he read 5 less books than he did in March. How many books did he read altogether in February, March and April?

   _____ books

4. Special certificates were given to students reading more than 10 books. In September 17 second graders received the certificate. In October there were 19, and in November there were 20 students. The certificates came in packages of 20. If they had 3 packages, how many certificates would be left over?

   _____ certificates

Book Store Sale

Name _____

Original Price	Discount
$1.00 — $2.99	$ .50 off
$3.00 — $5.99	$1.00 off
$6.00 — $8.99	$1.50 off
$9.00 and over	$2.00 off

The book store at the mall is having a special sale. If you choose a book that is marked $9.95, you can subtract $2.00 and buy it for just $7.95. Figure out how much you would spend if you made the following purchases.

1. You choose two books originally priced at $2.95 each.

   _____ sale price

2. You choose one book originally priced at $3.95 and one book at $5.95.

   _____ sale price

3. You choose one book originally priced at $4.95 and one book at $7.95.

   _____ sale price

4. You choose one book originally priced at $8.50 and one book at $4.95.

   _____ sale price

© Taylor & Francis Group • *Math Extension Units Book 1*

Collection Fair

Name _____

The children at Briar Glen School were having a Collection Fair. The children brought their collections or hobbies to school and displayed them on tables in the gym. The tickets to the fair cost $1.25 for adults and $.75 for children.

1. Nancy, Sara, and Ashley each brought their sticker collections. Nancy had 32 stickers. Jill had 18 more than Nancy. Sara had the same number as Jill. How many stickers did they have altogether?

   _____ stickers

2. Mr. and Mrs. Anderson, their 3 sons and 2 daughters came to the fair. How much change would Mr. Anderson get back from $10.00 after buying tickets for all of them?

   _____ change

3. Chuck, Larry, and Sabe each brought their baseball cards. Chuck had 47 cards, Larry had 53 cards, and Sabe had 60 cards. If they share a table and put their cards together in rows of 20, how many rows of 20 were they able to make?

   _____ rows

4. Brandon was at the fair from 9:15 am to 12:45 p.m. His best friend Doug came to the fair at 8:45 am and left at 11:45 am. Which boy stayed longer at the fair and how much longer?

   _____ stayed   _____ minutes longer

Fast Food Restaurant

Name _____

Maria, Carlos, and their parents stopped at their favorite fast food restaurant on their way to the shopping center. This is the restaurant's menu.

Menu

Burgers	$.70	Cookies	$.50
Cheeseburgers	$.80	Ice Cream	$.75
Hot Dogs	$.55	Cherry Pie	$.90
Fries	$.85	Small Drink	$.60
Curly Fries	$.90	Medium Drink	$.80
Potato Chips	$.50	Large Drink	$1.00

1. Maria ordered a burger, fries, a medium drink, and a cookie. Carlos ordered a cheeseburger, curly fries, a large drink, and ice cream. Whose order cost more? How much more?

   _____'s order cost _____ more

2. Their father ordered two burgers, fries, a large drink, and a cherry pie. Their mother ordered a hot dog, chips, a medium drink, and ice cream. Their father's order cost how much more than their mother's?

   _____ more

3. Their father paid for all four meals by giving the cashier a $5.00 bill and a $10.00 bill. How much change did he get?

   _____ change

4. How much would the cheapest and the most expensive meals you could choose cost if you included a sandwich, some kind of potato, a drink, and a dessert?

   cheapest_____   most expensive_____

School Store

Name _____

The students in Mrs. Becker's class went to the Mill Street School Store every Friday morning. It was always fun for the children to buy supplies such as markers, pencils, crayons, glue, erasers, and notebooks.

MARKERS
$2.50

GLUE
75¢

PENCIL
10¢

NOTEBOOK
$1.25

CRAYONS
$1.50

ERASER
20¢

1. Audrey had $3.85. If she bought crayons, 2 pencils and glue, how much money would she have left?

   $_____

2. Eileen had 3 quarters, 2 dimes, and 1 nickel. How much more money does she need to buy a notebook, eraser, and glue?

   $_____

3. If Linda gave the storekeeper $2.00, what is the fewest number of coins she could get back in change if she bought a notebook, eraser, and pencil?

   _____ coins

4. Kyle and Kelly are twins in Mrs. Becker's class. Their mother gave them $7.00 to spend at the store. Kyle bought an eraser, glue, and a notebook. Kelly bought markers, crayons, and 3 pencils. How much more did Kelly spend than Kyle?

   $_____ more

Speedy Delivery

Name_____

Mr. Brown drives a truck for the Speedy Delivery Service located in Oakton. He picks up and delivers packages in towns within 50 miles of Oakton. He always tries to take the shortest route to get from town to town.

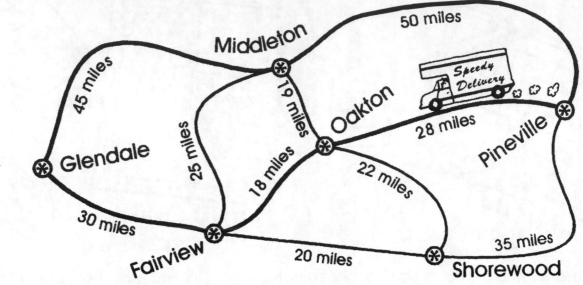

1. How far did Mr. Brown drive from the office in Oakton to pick up packages in Glendale, if he took the shortest route?

   _____ miles

2. He picked up two packages in Glendale. One was to be delivered to Middleton and one to Shorewood. What would be the shortest route to deliver both packages?

   Glendale to _____ to _____ to _____

3. How much farther is it from Pineville to Middleton to Fairview than from Pineville to Shorewood to Fairview?

   _____ miles farther

   How many miles is the shortest route from Pineville to Fairview? _____ miles

4. How far is it from Pineville to Glendale, taking the shortest route? _____ miles

Field Day

Name _____

Hartford Hills School held their field day last Saturday. Each grade had one team. The intermediate grades (4, 5, and 6) competed against each other and the primary grades (1, 2, and 3) competed against each other.

1. The fourth grade had 12 girls and 14 boys on their team. The fifth grade had 9 girls and 16 boys. The 6th grade had 10 girls and 14 boys. How many more boys than girls in the intermediate grades took part in field day?

   _____ more

2. The first grade scored 15 points in relays, 16 points in ball toss, and 25 points in long jump. They had 6 points more than the second grade's total. How many points did the second grade score altogether?

   _____ points

3. The fifth grade won in the intermediate division. They scored 66 points. This was 5 points more than the fourth grade and 2 points more than the sixth grade. How many points did all three grades score together?

   _____ points.

4. In the jog-walk the second grade scored 2 points more than the first grade and 5 points less than the third grade. Together, all three grades scored a total of 21 in this event. What was each grade's score?

   1st grade _____   2nd grade _____   3rd grade _____

Assignment Sheet

Name _____

I began this unit on money on _____ (date).

Mark off each activity after you have completed it and after it has been checked.
Hand in all pages when you finish the unit.

Lesson	Completed	Checked
1. Counting Money	_____	_____
2. Using Money Symbols	_____	_____
3. Trading Coins	_____	_____
4. Different Ways	_____	_____
5. Ways to Make 25 Cents	_____	_____
6. Ways to Make 30 Cents	_____	_____
7. Ways to Make 35 Cents	_____	_____
8. Making Change	_____	_____
9. Piggy Bank Logic	_____	_____
10. More Piggy Bank Problems	_____	_____
11. Ten Coins in the Bank	_____	_____
12. Problem Solving	_____	_____
13. Money Pictures	_____	_____

I completed the unit on _____ (date).

Counting Money

Name _____

1. Write the three numbers that would come next when counting pennies.

    25¢, 26¢, _____¢, _____¢, _____¢

2. Write the three numbers that would come next when counting nickels.

    30¢, 35¢, _____¢, _____¢, _____¢

3. Write the three numbers that would come next when counting dimes.

    30¢, 40¢, _____¢, _____¢, _____¢

4. Write the three numbers that would come next when counting quarters.

    25¢, 50¢, _____¢, _____¢, _____¢

5. Write the three numbers that would come next when counting half dollars.

    50¢, 100¢, _____¢, _____¢, _____¢

When we count coins we usually start with the highest valued coins, then count the next highest valued coins, and so on. For example, we would start with the quarters, then the dimes, and then the nickels and pennies.

6. If you were counting out 2 quarters, 2 dimes and 4 pennies, you would say

    25¢, 50¢, 60¢, 70¢, 71¢, _____¢, _____¢, _____¢

Write the numbers you would say when counting these coins.

7. 1 quarter, 3 dimes, 2 nickels   25¢, 35¢ ____ ____ ____ ____

8. 1 half dollar, 1 quarter, 1 dime, 1 nickel   ____ ____ ____ ____

9. 5 dimes, 3 nickels   ____ ____ ____ ____ ____ ____ ____ ____

Using Money Symbols

Name _____

There are different symbols or signs we use to show money. When the amount is less than one dollar, we usually use the cents sign (¢).

When the amount is one dollar or more, we usually use the dollar sign ($) and a decimal point (.) to divide the dollars and cents.

$1.00 is one dollar and zero cents $2.05 is two dollars and five cents

Write the amounts below using cents signs or dollar signs and decimal points.

1. 95 cents _____   7. 10 dollars and 12 cents _____

2. 1 dollar and 50 cents _____   8. 12 dollars and 10 cents _____

3. 2 dollars and 25 cents_____   9. 15 dollars and 5 cents_____

4. 45 cents _____   10. 45 dollars _____

5. 9 dollars and 95 cents_____   11. 25 dollars and 75 cents _____

6. 5 dollars _____   12. 5 cents _____

Sometimes in stores or in advertisements they use the dollar sign ($) but the leave out the decimal point. They use smaller numbers to show the cents. In the prices below the big numbers stand for the dollars and small numbers stand for the cents.

Write the prices using a dollar sign and a decimal point.

$6.25

Cakes	$4^{00}	_____
Wheat Bread	$1^{95}	_____
Pies	$3^{75}	_____
Rye Bread	$2^{05}	_____

Trading Coins

Name _____

The object of this game below is to trade the coins in Box A for the fewest number of coins you can using quarters, dimes, nickels, and pennies. You must still have the same value when you are finished trading.

Fewest Number Coins Trading Game		
Box A - Coins at the Beginning	**Box B** - Coins After Trading	
Example 1 dime _25¢_ 15 pennies _16_ coins	1 quarter _25¢_ _1_ coin	
4 nickels 7 pennies ____¢ ____coins	____ quarters ____ dimes ____ nickels ____ pennies	____¢ ____ coins
4 dimes 3 nickels 5 pennies ____¢ ____coins	____ quarters ____ dimes ____ nickels ____ pennies	____¢ ____ coins
1 quarter 3 dimes 2 nickels 6 pennies ____¢ ____coins	____ quarters ____ dimes ____ nickels ____ pennies	____¢ ____ coins
5 dimes 8 nickels 3 pennies ____¢ ____coins	____ quarters ____ dimes ____ nickels ____ pennies	____¢ ____ coins
6 dimes 3 nickels 10 pennies ____¢ ____coins	____ quarters ____ dimes ____ nickels ____ pennies	____¢ ____ coins

Different Ways

Name _____

There are several different ways to make 10 cents. For example, you could use a dime, 2 nickels or 1 nickel and 5 pennies.

Fill in the charts to show all the ways you could make 10¢ and 15¢ and 20¢.

Ways to make 10¢

Dime	Nickel	Penny
1	0	0
0	2	0
0	1	5

Ways to make 15¢

Dime	Nickel	Penny
1	1	0

Ways to make 20¢

Dime	Nickel	Penny
2		

Ways to Make 25 Cents

Name _____

There are 12 different ways to make 25¢
using dimes, nickels, and pennies.
Fill in the chart below showing all the
different ways to make 25¢.

Hint: Make an organized list
- First show all the ways of using 2 dimes.
- Then show all the ways of using 1 dime.
- Next use 0 dimes.

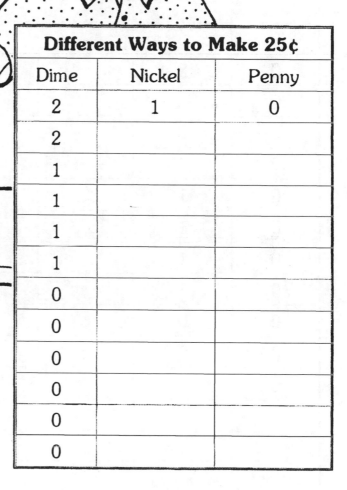

Different Ways to Make 25¢		
Dime	Nickel	Penny
2	1	0
2		
1		
1		
1		
1		
0		
0		
0		
0		
0		
0		

Ways to Make 30 Cents

Name _____

There are 18 different ways to make 30 cents using quarters, dimes, nickels, and pennies. The chart below is the beginning of an organized list that shows all the possible ways to make 30 cents. Some of the boxes have been filled in for you. Fill in the rest of the boxes to complete the chart.

Different Ways to Make 30¢			
Quarter	Dime	Nickel	Penny
1	0	1	0
1			
0	3		
0	2		
0	2		
0	2		
0			
0	1		
0	1		
0	1		
0	1		
0	0	6	
0	0	5	
0	0	4	

Ways to Make 35 Cents

Name _____

Make an organized list to show all the possible ways of making 35¢ using quarters, dimes, nickels, and pennies.

Hint

- Start with all the possible ways using one quarter.
- Then list all the ways using 3 dimes.
- Next list all the ways using 2 dimes.
- Next list all the ways using 1 dime.
- Last, list all the ways using 0 dimes.

Different Ways to Make 35¢			
Quarters	Dimes	Nickels	Pennies

Making Change

Name _____

Imagine you are the cashier giving your customers change. You always give change using the fewest possible coins. For each amount shown in the chart below, show what coins you would give in change.

Amount of Change to be given	Quarters	Dimes	Nickels	Pennies
15¢	0	1	1	0
40¢				
22¢				
38¢				
55¢				
46¢				
77¢				
33¢				
60¢				
75¢				
59¢				
90¢				
74¢				
59¢				
95¢				
62¢				
41¢				
80¢				
27¢				
68¢				
19¢				

Piggy Bank Logic

Name _____

1. I have 4 coins in my piggy bank.
   One coin is a nickel. One coin is
   less than a nickel. I have less
   than 40¢ altogether. How many
   of each coin do I have.

Quarters	Dimes	Nickels	Pennies

How much money do I have in my bank? _____

2. I have 6 coins in my piggy bank. None of them is a nickel. Three (3) of them are
   worth more than a nickel. I have 2 more pennies than I have quarters. How
   many of each coin do I have?

Quarters	Dimes	Nickels	Pennies

How much money do I have in my bank? _____

3. I have 8 coins in my piggy bank. I have twice as many dimes as I have quarters. I
   have twice as many pennies as I have dimes. I have less than 95¢ altogether.
   How many of each coin I have?

Quarters	Dimes	Nickels	Pennies

How much money do I have in my bank? _____

More Piggy Bank Problems

Name _____

1. I have an equal number of quarters, dimes, nickels, and pennies in my piggy bank. I have more than 50¢ but less than $1.00. How many of each coin do I have?

Quarters	Dimes	Nickels	Pennies

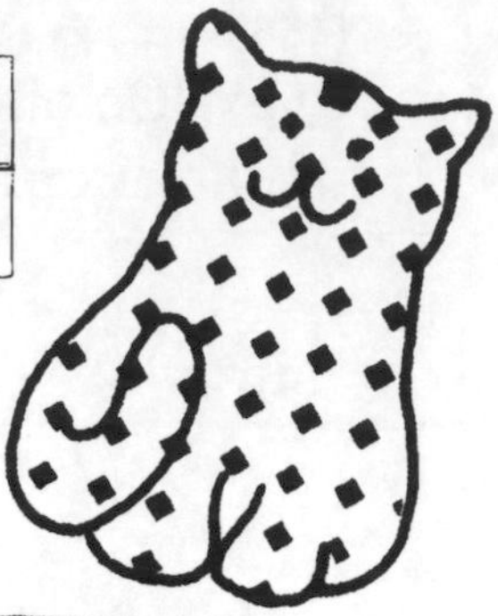

How much money do I have in my bank? _____

2. I have 7 coins in my piggy bank. I have 1 more nickel than I have dimes. I have the same number of quarters and pennies. I have less than 70¢. Fill in the chart below to show how many of each coin do I have?

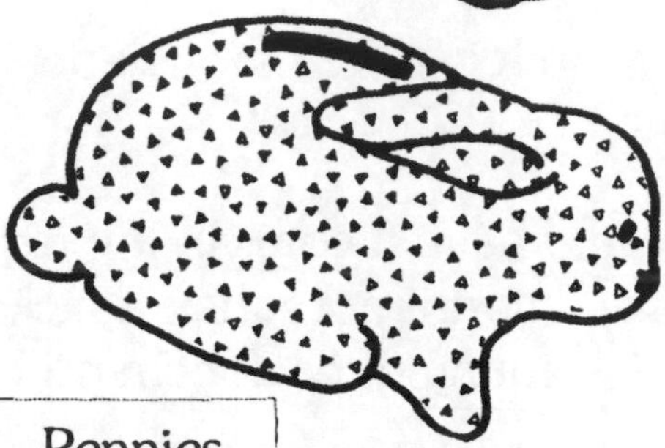

Quarters	Dimes	Nickels	Pennies

How much money do I have in my bank? _____

3. I have 8 coins in my piggy bank. I have no nickels. I have 3 more pennies than I have quarters. I have twice as many quarters as I have dimes. I have less than $1.00. How many of each coin do I have?

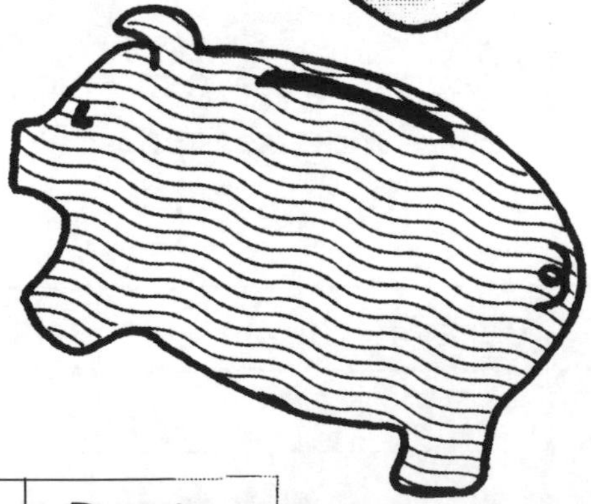

Quarters	Dimes	Nickels	Pennies

How much money do I have in my bank? _____

TEN COINS IN THE BANK

Name _____

Pretend you have 10 coins that equal the different amounts shown in the chart below. You have no quarters or half dollars. Fill in the chart to show how many dimes, nickels and pennies you have. **Hint**: You may need to use play money to figure out what the 10 coins are.

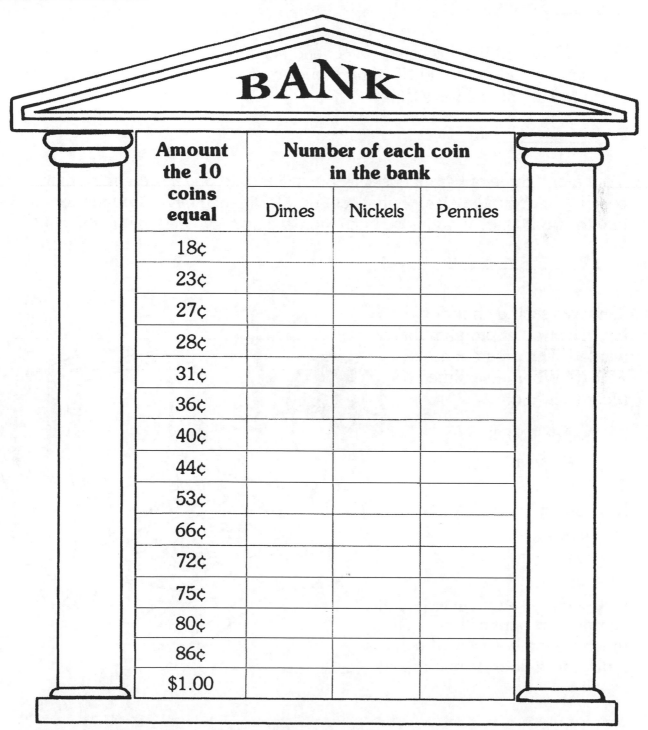

Amount the 10 coins equal	Number of each coin in the bank		
	Dimes	Nickels	Pennies
18¢			
23¢			
27¢			
28¢			
31¢			
36¢			
40¢			
44¢			
53¢			
66¢			
72¢			
75¢			
80¢			
86¢			
$1.00			

Problem Solving

Name _____

1. Janella had $1.00 to spend at the candy store. She bought a candy bar for 40¢, gum drops for 15¢, gum for 30¢, and a candy stick for 10¢. How much change did she get?

   _____ ¢ change

2. Michael had $2.20 in his bank. He got another $2.00 in a valentine from his grandmother. He spent $1.25 of his money on a valentine for his mother. How much money did he have left?

   $ _____ left

3. Tonda and three of her friends each put in $1.25 to buy a present for their coach. They found a nice gift that cost $6.00. Did they have enough money to buy the $6.00 gift? If not, how much more would they need to buy the gift?

   _____

4. Rajiv was saving his money to buy a computer program that he wanted. The program costs $19.75. When he counted his money he had:

1	five dollar bill
7	one dollar bills
1	half dollar
12	quarters
15	dimes
20	nickels
80	pennies

   Does he have enough to buy the computer program? If so, how much will he have left? If not, how much more does he need? _____

Money Pictures

Name _____

In the following pictures, all circles are worth 10¢. All squares are worth 5¢. All rectangles are worth 25¢. All triangles are worth 1¢. Find the cost of each picture.

(10¢) [5¢] [25¢] /1¢\

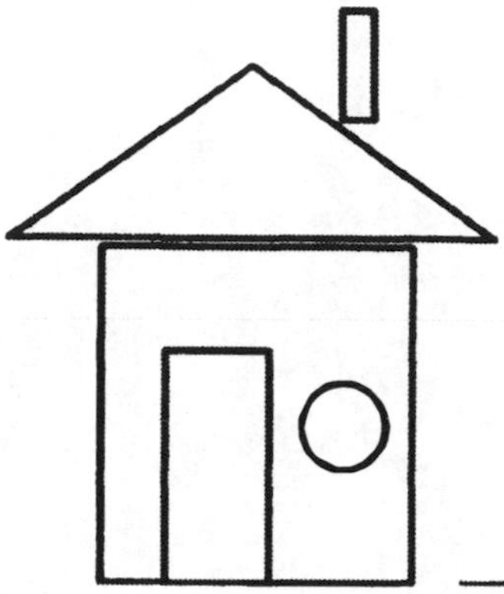

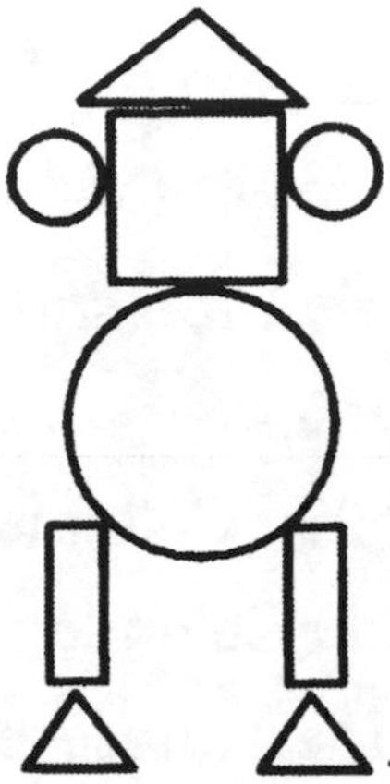

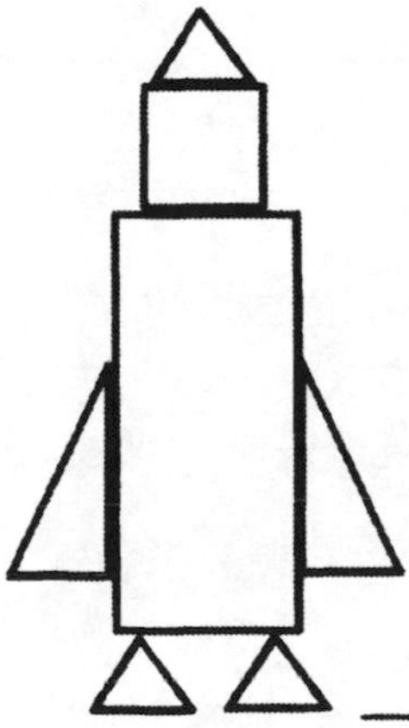

Make your own drawings with the prices that are shown.

37¢   58¢   26¢

Assignment Sheet

Name _____

I began this unit on time and measurement on _____ (date).

Mark off each activity after you have completed it and after it has been checked. Hand in all the pages when you finish the unit.

Lesson	Completed	Checked
1. Digital and Analog Clocks	_____	_____
2. Minutes Before and After the Hour	_____	_____
3. Timely Problems	_____	_____
4. Play Time	_____	_____
5. Monthly Calendar	_____	_____
6. Yearly Calendar	_____	_____
7. Temperatures Above Zero	_____	_____
8. Temperatures Below Zero	_____	_____
9. Liquid Measurements	_____	_____
10. Ways to Make a Gallon	_____	_____
11. Container Capers	_____	_____
12. Party Punch	_____	_____

I completed the unit on _____ (date).

Digital and Analog Clocks

Name _____

People need to be able to tell time on both digital and analog clocks. Draw the hour hand and the minute hand to match the time shown on the digital clock. On the line below the clocks, write an activity that you might be doing at each of these times.

A. M.

Activity _Leaving for school_

1. **P. M.**

Activity _____

4. **P. M.**

Activity _____

2. **Noon**

Activity _____

5. **P. M.**

Activity _____

3. **A. M.**

Activity _____

6. **P. M.**

Activity _____

Minutes Before and After the Hour

Name _____

There are 60 minutes in every
hour. When we write time, we
show how many minutes past
the hour. For example the clocks
on the right show 25 minutes
past the hour of six and also 35
minutes until seven o'clock.

Read each clock below and tell how many minutes until the next hour.

1. **3:50**

_____ minutes until __ o'clock

4.

_____ minutes until ___ o'clock

2.

_____ minutes until ___ o'clock

5. **4:40**

_____ minutes until ___ o'clock

3. **10:55**

_____ minutes until __ o'clock

6.

_____ minutes until ___ o'clock

Timely Problems

Name _____

Answer the questions below. Be sure to indicate a.m. and p.m. in your answers.

1. Mother tells Maria that Grandpa and Grandma Martinez will arrive in three hours. If it is 11:00 a.m., what time will they arrive? _____

2. If Blair left her house at 2:45 p.m. and arrived at her friend's house 15 minutes later, what time did Blair arrive at her friend's house? _____

3. Ronnie started reading his book at 4:30 p.m. He read for one hour and 30 minutes. What time was it when he stopped reading? _____

4. It takes Norma one half an hour to walk around the neighborhood park. If she finishes at 2:00 p.m., what time did she start? _____

5. Brandon starts opening his birthday presents at 1:20 p.m. and finishes at 2:00 p.m. How many minutes does it take him to open his presents?_____

6. Thomas' family drove to Orlando on their vacation. It took 5 hours to drive. If they left at 6:00 a.m., what time did they arrive? _____

7. My school starts at _____ a.m.

   My school ends at _____ p.m.

   My school day is _____ hours and _____ minutes long.

8. Ashley's piano lesson starts at 4:10 p.m. If her lesson is 45 minutes long, what time will her lesson be over? _____

Play Time

Name _____

The Children's Theater presents several children's plays throughout the day. Check the schedule and determine the length of each play and answer the following questions.

1. The Jack and the Beanstalk play
   is _____ minutes long.

2. The Hansel and Gretel play
   is _____ minutes long.

3. The Little Red Riding Hood play
   is _____ minutes long.

4. The Three Little Pigs play
   is _____ minutes long.

5. The Little Red Hen play
   is _____ minutes long.

6. The Three Bears
   is _____ minutes long.

Children's Theater Schedule

Hansel and Gretel
9:23 - 10:00 a.m.

Little Red Riding Hood
10:10 - 10:45 a.m.

The Three Bears
10:48 - 11:30 a.m.

The Three Pigs
11:34 - 12:21 p.m.

Jack and the Beanstalk
12:49 - 1:29 p.m.

LITTLE RED HEN
1:45 - 2:18 p.m.

7. Which play is the longest? _____

8. Which play is the shortest? _____

9. If you have to leave the theater by 10:50 a.m., which play or plays could you see?

_____

10. If you are not able to arrive at the theater before 12:15 p.m., which play or plays

could you see? _____

Monthly Calendar

Name _____

November

Sun	Mon	Tue	Wed	Thu	Fri	Sat
			1	2	Christina's Birthday 3	4
5	6	Election Day 7	8	9	10	11
12	13	14	15	Mark's Birthday 16	17	18
19	20	21	22	Thanksgiving 23	24	25
26	27	28	29	30		

A monthly calendar shows time. It helps us count the days and the weeks in a month.

Use the calendar to answer the following questions.

1. How many days are in the month of November? _____

2. How many Wednesdays are in November? _____

3. How many Saturdays are in November? _____

4. What day of the week is Christina's birthday? _____

5. How many days from Christina's birthday until Mark's birthday? _____

6. How many days are there from Election Day to Thanksgiving? _____

7. What is the date three weeks after Election Day? _____

8. What is the date of the third Saturday in November? _____

9. What happens one week after Mark's birthday? _____

10. What is the date one week after Thanksgiving? _____

11. What is the date of the first Thursday? _____

12. What is the date of the fourth Monday? _____

13. November 24th is how many weeks after Christina's birthday? _____

14. How many days are there in 2 weeks? _____ in 3 weeks? _____

15. How many Tuesdays are there between November 8 and November 22? _____

Yearly Calendar

Name _____

January	February	March	April	May	June
July	August	September	October	November	December

A yearly calendar helps us keep track of the days and months in a year. Use the yearly calendar above to answer the following questions.

1. How many months are in a year? _____

2. What is the first month of the year? _____

   the 6th month? _____   the 10th month? _____

3. If Martha's birthday is in October and her brother's birthday is 3 months earlier, what month is her brother's birthday? _____

4. If it is Vanessa's job to feed the dog every other month and she starts feeding him in January, what is the 3rd month she will feed the dog? _____

5. Aunt Sherrie and Uncle John came to visit in April and they said they would come back in July. How many months until they return? _____

6 Dad bought the airline tickets for the family's June vacation three months before they left. What month did Dad buy the tickets? _____

7. Chuck let his brother Douglas use his room while he was away at college. How many months will Douglas get to use the room if Chuck leaves for college on September 1st and returns at the end of May? _____

8. Carol's birthday is July 25th and Christmas is December 25th. How many months before Christmas is Carol's birthday? _____

Temperatures Above Zero

Name _____

A thermometer is an instrument used to measure the degrees of coldness and hotness (temperature). Temperature can be measured using a scale marked in degrees Fahrenheit. Use the four thermometers to answer the questions.

A 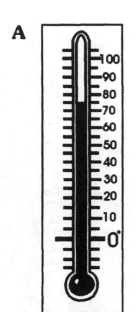   **B** 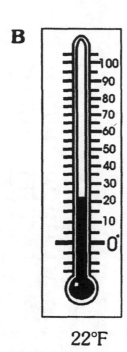   **C** 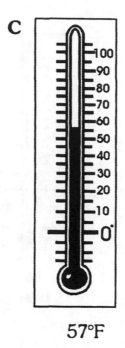   **D**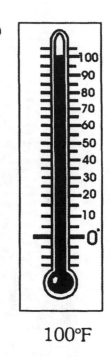

75°F   22°F   57°F   100°F

1. Look at thermometer **A**. What would the temperature be if it
   dropped 15 degrees?_____   went up 12 degrees?_____

2. Look at thermometer **B**. What would the temperature be if it
   dropped 15 degrees?_____   went up 12 degrees?_____

3. Look at thermometer **C**. What would the temperature be if it
   dropped 15 degrees?_____ went up 12 degrees?_____

4. Look at thermometer **D**. What would the temperature be if it
   dropped 15 degrees?_____   went up 12 degrees?_____

5. 32° is the freezing point. How many degrees below freezing is the temperature
   on thermometer **B**?_____

6. How many degrees above freezing is thermometer C?_____   D?_____

Temperatures Below Zero

Name _____

A thermometer measures the degrees of temperature above and below zero. As the temperature drops below zero, we write the number of degrees below zero using a negative number. For example, if the temperature is 5 degrees below 0°F it is written -5°F.

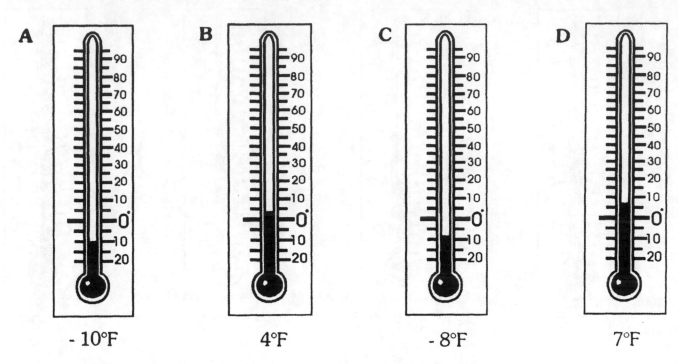

- 10°F   4°F   - 8°F   7°F

Use the thermometers above to answer the following questions.

1. Look at thermometer **A**. What would the temperature be if it
   dropped 15 degrees?_____   went up 12 degrees?_____

2. Look at thermometer **B**. What would the temperature be if it
   dropped 15 degrees?_____   went up 12 degrees?_____

3. Look at thermometer **C**. What would the temperature be if it
   dropped 15 degrees?_____   went up 12 degrees?_____

4. Look at thermometer **D**. What would the temperature be if it
   dropped 15 degrees?_____   went up 12 degrees?_____

5. 32° is the freezing point. How many degrees below freezing is the temperature on
   thermometer C?_____

Liquid Measurements
Less Than a Gallon

Name _____

2 cups = 1 pint   2 quarts = 1/2 gallon
2 pints = 1 quart   4 quarts = 1 gallon

1. This chart shows 3 different ways to
   measure 1 quart. Fill in the chart to
   show another way to make 1 quart.

Quarts	Pints	Cups
1	0	0
0	2	0
0	1	2

2. How many different ways can you
   make 1/2 gallon? Fill in the blank
   spaces on the chart.

Quarts	Pints	Cups
2	0	0
1	2	0
1		2
1		
	4	
		2
0		
		6
	0	

Circle either "greater than" or "less than"
in each sentence to make the sentence true.

1. 1 quart is (greater than / less than)
   3 pints.

2. 5 pints is (greater than / less than)
   1 quart.

3. 3 cups is (greater than / less than) 1 pint.

4. 7 cups is (greater than / less than)
   1/2 gallon.

5. 3 pints and 3 cups is (greater than / less
   than) 1/2 gallon.

6. 1 quart and 1 pint and 1 cup is (greater
   than / less than) 1/2 gallon.

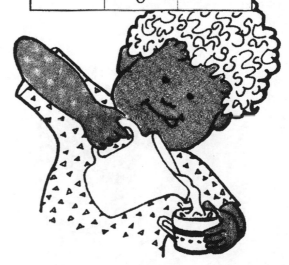

Ways to Make a Gallon

Name _____

2 cups = 1 pint
2 pints = 1 quart
2 quarts = 1/2 gallon
4 quarts = 1 gallon

How many different ways can you make 1 gallon? Complete the chart on the right.

1. How many different ways can you make 1 gallon using only quarts and pints?

   _____

2. How many different ways can you make 1 gallon using only pints and cups?

   _____

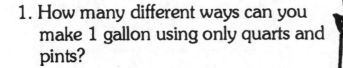

Quarts	Pints	Cups
4	0	0
3	2	0
3	1	2
3	0	4
2		0
2		2
2	2	
	1	6
2		
1		0
	5	2
1		4
		6
		8
1		
0		0
	6	4
0		
		10
	2	

Container Capers

Name _____

1 gallon
- 4 quarts
- 3 quarts
- 2 quarts
- 1 quart

1 quart
- 4 cups
- 3 cups
- 2 cups
- 1 cup

1 pint
- 2 cups
- 1 cup

Containers

A B C D E

1. **Container A** holds 1 pint and 2 cups. How many quarts does it hold? _____

2. **Container B** holds 1 pint and 10 cups. How many quarts does it hold? _____

3. **Container C** holds 5 pints and 6 cups. How many quarts does it hold? _____

4. **Container D** holds 1 quart, 1 pint, and 2 cups. How many quarts does is hold?

_____

5. **Container E** holds 6 pints, 4 cups, 1 quart. How many quarts does it hold? _____

6. Which container will hold the most amount? _____ the least amount ? _____

7. Which container will hold 10 pints of punch? _____

8. Which container will hold more than 1 gallon of punch? _____

9. Which container will hold a half gallon of punch? _____

10. Which container will hold exactly hold 1 gallon? _____

Party Punch

Name _____

1 pint = 2 cups
1 quart = 2 pints
1 quart = 4 cups
1 gallon = 4 quarts
1 gallon = 8 pints

The children in Ms. Strum's class want to make a punch for their Valentine's Day party. This is the recipe they will use.

Party Punch

4 quarts fruit juice
6 pints lemon-lime soda
1/2 gallon apple juice

1. The recipe needs

_____ pints (or _____ cups) of fruit juice

_____ pints (or _____ cups) of lemon-lime soda

_____ pints (or _____ cups) of apple juice

2. The party punch recipe needs _____ more pints of fruit juice than lemon-lime soda pop.

3. How many pints of punch does the recipe make? _____ pints

4. How many total cups of punch does the recipe make? _____ cups

5. Would there be enough punch to serve 1 cup to each of the 25 students in the class and 1 teacher? _____

6. How many students in the class could have 2 cups? _____

Answers

Place Value

The Importance of Place - pg. 8

1. b. 7,546   d. 5,927   c. 8,350
2. a. 800,   5
   b. 90   7,000
      2   300
   c. 3   40
      600   2,000
   d. 200   0
      8,000   70
   e. 4,000   500
      0   9

Understanding Place Value - pg. 9

1. 6,043   8. 7,418
2. 6,043   9. 2,907; 1,900
3. 8,136   10. 3,782
4. 1,879   11. 1,879
5. 2,907   12. 9,590
6. 5,264; 5,624   13. 8,136; 4,625; 2,907
7. 4,625   2,351; 6,043

Different Ways - pg. 10

1. 2,589; 9,852
2. 7,531; 1,357
3. 635, 653, 536, 563, 365, 356
4. 4,763; 4,367; 6,743; 6,347
5. 5,023; 5,032; 5,203; 5,230; 5,320; 5,302

Number Pyramid - pg. 11

1. 413   9. 6,336
2. 432   10. 797
3. 4,867   11. 83
4. 1,937   12. 302
5. 347   13. 3,965
6. 28   14. 9,02
7. 1,860   15. 1,513
8. 495

Place Value Scramble - pg. 12

1. 1,839   7. 2,431
2. 4,762   8. 250
3. 3,570   9. 8,215
4. 7,126   10. 9023
5. 6,905   11. 10,325
6. 5,348

Finding Mystery Numbers - pg. 13

Robbie's number = 11
1. 34
2. 80
3. 110

What's My Mystery Number? - pg. 14

1. 6   4. 3
2. 11   5. 14
3. 16   6. 18

What's My Mystery Number? - pg. 15

1. 48   4. 64
2. 77   5. 30
3. 36   6. 95

What's My Mystery Number)? - pg. 16

1. 155   3. 909
2. 642   4. 234

Really Big Numbers - pg. 17

1. 195,267   5. 231,250
2. 304,690   6. 29,542
3. 210,175   7. 705,100
4. 562,068   8. 8,075

More or Less - pg. 18

1. Answers will vary but should be greater than 500,000
2. Answers will vary but should be less than 500,000
3. a. 6,280   g. 790,595
   b. 1,762   h. 750,750
   c. 15,600   i. 455,675
   d. 75,450   j. 592,500
   e. 155,680   k. 784,653
   f. 485,000   l. 563,748
Bonus - 1,000,000

Largest to Smallest - pg. 19

527,289 (largest)   257,145
437,289   23,794
311,712   14,393
310,712   14,294

Problem Solving and Computational Application

Jessie's Valentine Party - pg. 21

1. 3 invitations   3. 18 scoops
2. 2 favors   4. team 2; 10 points

The Amusement Park - pg. 22

1. 6 hours   3. 1 ride
2. $34.00   4. $1.50

Trip to the Farm - pg. 23

1. 10 apples   3. 6 people
2. 6 cups   4. 10 pounds

A Day at the Beach - pg. 24

1. 10 shells   3. 12 shells
2. Mrs. Romano; 2 min.   4. 10 slices

George's Party - pg. 25

1. 4 holders   3. 45 minutes
2. 2 napkins   4. $.50

Playing Darts - pg. 26

Tonya - 30, 50, 35, 115 - winner
Kevin - 45, 25, 40, 110
Bonus - 2 red, 2 black
    1 red, 1 yellow, 1 blue, 1 black
    1 red, 2 blue, 1 green
    2 yellow, 2 blue
    1 red, 1 yellow, 2 green
    1 red, 2 blue, 1 green
    2 red, 2 black

Reading Club - pg. 27

1. 20 books
2. 5 packages, 2 boxes
3. 33 books
4. 4 certificates

Book Store Sale - pg. 28

1. $4.90
2. $7.90
3. $10.40
4. $10.95

Collection Fair - pg. 29

1. 132
2. $3.75
3. 8
4. Brandon; 30 min.

Fast Food - pg. 30

1. Carlos; 60¢
2. $1.55
3. $1.95
4. $2.15; $3.60

School Store - pg. 31

1. $1.40
2. $1.20
3. 3 (1 quarter, 2 dimes)
4. $2.10

Speedy Delivery - pg. 32

1. 48
2. Middleton to Oakton to Shorewood
3. 20; 46
4. 76

Field Day - pg. 33

1. 13 more boys
2. 50 points
3. 191 points
4. 1st- 4; 2nd - 6; 3rd - 11

Money

Counting Money - pg. 35

1. 27, 28 29
2. 40, 45, 50
3. 50, 60, 70
4. 75, 100, 125
5. 150, 200 250
6. 72, 73, 74
7. 25, 35, 45, 55, 60, 65
8. 50, 75, 85, 90
9. 10, 20, 30, 40, 50, 55, 60, 65

Using Money Symbols - pg. 36

1. 95¢ or $.95
2. $1.50
3. $2.25
4. 45¢ or $.45
5. $9.95
6. $5.00
7. $10.12
8. $12.10
9. $15.05
10. $45.00
11. $25.75
12. 5¢ or $.05
cakes - $4.00
pies - $3.75
wheat bread - $1.95
rye bread - $2.05

Trading Coins - pg. 37

Box A	Box B
27¢, 11 coins	1 quarter
	2 pennies
	27¢, 3 coins
60¢, 12 coins	2 q
	1 d
	60¢, 3 coins
71¢, 12 coins	2 q
	2 d
	1 p
	71¢, 5 coins
93¢, 16 coins	3 q
	1 d
	1 n
	3 p
	93¢, 8 coins
85¢, 19 coins	3 q
	1 d
	85¢, 4 coins

Different Ways - pg. 38

see chart on page 64

Ways to Make 25 Cents - pg. 39

see chart on page 64

Ways to Make 30 Cents - pg. 40

see chart on page 64

Ways to Make 35 Cents - pg. 41

see chart on page 64

Making Change - pg. 42

see chart on page 65

Piggy Bank Logic - pg. 43

1. 2 dimes, 1 nickel 1 penny; 26¢
2. 1 quarter, 2 dimes, 3 pennies; 48¢
3. 1 quarter, 2 dimes, 1 nickel, 4 pennies; 54¢

More Piggy Bank Problems - pg. 44

1. 2 quarters, 2 dimes, 2 nickels, 2 pennies; 82¢
2. 1 quarter, 2 dimes, 3 nickels, 1 penny; 61¢
3. 2 quarters, 1 dime, 5 pennies; 65¢

Ten Coins - pg. 45

	dimes	nickels	pennies
18¢	0	2	8
23¢	1	1	8
27¢	1	2	7
28¢	2	0	8
31¢	1	3	6
36¢	2	2	6
40¢	2	3	5
44¢	2	4	4
53¢	3	4	3
66¢	4	5	1
72¢	6	2	2
75¢	5	5	0
80¢	6	4	0

Ten Coins, continued

| 86¢ | 8 | 1 | 1 |
| $1.00 | 10 | 0 | 0 |

Problem Solving - pg. 46

1. 5
2. $2.95
3. no, $1.00
4. no, 95¢

Money Pictures - pg. 47

snowman - 41¢   house - 66¢
robot - 88¢   rocket - 35¢
engine - $1.11   boat - $1.26
Answers will vary.

Time and Measurement

Digital and Analog Clocks - pg. 49

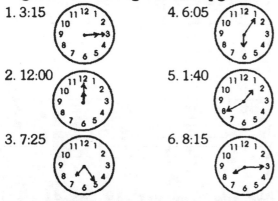

1. 3:15
2. 12:00
3. 7:25
4. 6:05
5. 1:40
6. 8:15

Minutes Before and After the Hour - pg. 50

1. 10 min., 4 o'clock
2. 25 min., 2 o'clock
3. 5 min., 11 o'clock
4. 35 min., 9 o'clock
5. 20 min., 5 o'clock
6. 45 min., 10 o'clock

Timely Problems - pg. 51

1. 2:00 p.m.
2. 3:00 p.m.
3. 6:00 p.m.
4. 1:30 p.m.
5. 40 minutes
6. 11:00 a.m.
7. answers will vary
8. 4:55 p.m.

Play Time - pg. 52

1. 40
2. 37
3. 35
4. 47
5. 33
6. 42
7. Three Pigs
8. Little Red Hen
9. Hansel and Gretel; Little Red Riding Hood
10. Jack and the Beanstalk; Little Red Hen

Monthly Calendar - pg. 53

1. 30 days
2. 5
3. 4
4. Friday
5. 13 days
6. 16 days
7. November 28
8. November 18
9. Thanksgiving
10. November 30
11. November 2
12. November 27
13. 3 weeks
14. 14 days; 21 days
15. 2

Yearly Calendar - pg. 54

1. 12 months
2. January, June, October
3. July
4. May
5. 3 months
6. March
7. 9 months
8. 5 months

Temperatures Above Zero - pg. 55

1. 60°, 87°
2. 7°, 34°
3. 42°, 69°
4. 85°, 112°
5. 10°
6. 25°, 68°

Temperatures Below Zero - pg. 56

1. -25°, 2°
2. -11°, 16°
3. -23°, 4°
4. -8°, 19°
5. 40°

Measurements Less than a Gallon - pg. 57

see charts on page 65
1. less than
2. greater than
3. greater than
4. less than
5. greater than
6. less than

Ways to Make a Gallon - pg. 58

see chart on page 65
1. 5
2. 9

Container Capers - pg. 59

1. 1 quart
2. 3 quarts
3. 4 quarts
4. 2 quarts
5. 5 quarts
6. most - E; least - A
7. E
8. E
9. D
10. C

Party Punch - pg. 60

1. 8 pints; 16 cups fruit juice
   6 pints; 12 cups soda
   4 pints; 8 cups apple juice
2. 2
3. 18
4. 36
5. yes
6. 10

Different Ways - pg. 38

10¢ Chart

Dime	Nickel	Penny
1	0	0
0	2	0
0	1	5
0	0	10

20¢ Chart

Dime	Nickel	Penny
2	0	0
1	2	0
1	1	5
1	0	10
0	4	0
0	3	5
0	2	10
0	1	15
0	0	20

15¢ Chart

Dime	Nickel	Penny
1	1	0
1	0	5
0	3	0
0	2	5
0	1	10
0	0	15

Ways to Make 25 Cents - pg. 39

Different Ways to Make 25¢		
Dime	Nickel	Penny
2	1	0
2	0	5
1	3	0
1	2	5
1	1	10
1	0	15
0	5	0
0	4	5
0	3	10
0	2	15
0	1	20
0	0	25

Ways to Make 30 Cents - pg. 40

Different Ways to Make 30¢			
Quarter	Dime	Nickel	Penny
1	0	1	0
1	0	0	5
0	3	0	0
0	2	2	0
0	2	1	5
0	2	0	10
0	1	4	0
0	1	3	5
0	1	2	10
0	1	1	15
0	1	0	20
0	0	6	0
0	0	5	5
0	0	4	10
0	0	3	15
0	0	2	20
0	0	1	25
0	0	0	30

Ways to Make 35 Cents - pg. 41

Different Ways to Make 35¢			
Quarters	Dimes	Nickels	Pennies
1	1	0	0
1	0	2	0
1	0	1	5
1	0	0	10
0	3	1	0
0	3	0	5
0	2	3	0
0	2	2	5
0	2	1	10
0	2	0	15
0	1	5	0
0	1	4	5
0	1	3	10
0	1	2	15
0	1	1	20
0	1	0	25
0	0	7	0
0	0	6	5
0	0	5	10
0	0	4	15
0	0	3	20
0	0	2	25
0	0	1	30
0	0	0	35

Making Change - pg. 42

Amount of Change to be given	Quarters	Dimes	Nickels	Pennies
15¢	0	1	1	0
40¢	1	1	1	0
22¢	0	2	0	2
38¢	1	1	0	3
55¢	2	0	1	0
46¢	1	2	0	1
77¢	3	0	0	2
33¢	1	0	1	3
60¢	2	1	0	0
75¢	3	0	0	0
59¢	2	0	1	4
90¢	3	1	1	0
74¢	2	2	0	4
59¢	2	0	1	4
95¢	3	2	0	0
62¢	2	1	0	2
41¢	1	1	1	1
80¢	3	0	1	0
27¢	1	0	0	2
68¢	2	1	1	3
19¢	0	1	1	4

Ways to Make a Gallon - pg. 58

Quarts	Pints	Cups
4	0	0
3	2	0
3	1	2
3	0	4
2	4	0
2	3	2
2	2	4
2	1	6
2	0	8
1	6	0
1	5	2
1	4	4
1	3	6
1	2	8
1	1	10
0	8	0
0	7	2
0	6	4
0	5	6
0	4	8
0	3	10
0	2	12
0	1	14
0	0	16

Measurements Less than a Gallon - pg. 57

Quarts	Pints	Cups
1	0	0
0	2	0
0	1	2
0	0	4

Quarts	Pints	Cups
2	0	0
1	2	0
1	1	2
1	0	4
0	4	0
0	3	2
0	2	4
0	1	6
0	0	8

Printed in the United States
by Baker & Taylor Publisher Services